T0346182

CAMBRIDGE
UNIVERSITY PRESS

University Printing House, Cambridge CB2 8BS, United Kingdom

Cambridge University Press is part of the University of Cambridge.

It furthers the University's mission by disseminating knowledge in the pursuit of
education, learning and research at the highest international levels of excellence.

www.cambridge.org
Information on this title: www.cambridge.org/9781316620076

© Cambridge University Press 1943

First published 1943
First paperback edition 2016

A catalogue record for this publication is available from the British Library

ISBN 978-1-316-62007-6 Paperback

PROSPECTS AND POLICIES

Five Speeches
on post-war subjects

by

The Rt Hon.
HERBERT MORRISON, M.P.

CAMBRIDGE
AT THE UNIVERSITY PRESS
1943

PREFATORY NOTE

During the last few months I have used some public occasions to outline certain ideas on post-war policy which, while they arise directly from my own political creed, seem to me to have a claim on the attention of open-minded people of all political parties or none. I have been gratified by the result, for the group of speeches in question seems to have aroused interest and discussion. A large number of requests have been received for the texts of the speeches, so when it was suggested that the Cambridge University Press might reproduce them in pamphlet form, I gladly agreed.

A much larger collection of my platform utterances since I have been a member of the Government is shortly to be published, under the title *Looking Forward*, by Messrs Hodder & Stoughton, who have very kindly placed no obstacle in the way of this present publication.

H. M.

1943

CONTENTS

I

SOCIAL AND ECONOMIC POLICY[1]

FOR several years the British people have been passing through great experiences. They have borne themselves greatly in face of them. For what they knew was right, they entered this war and challenged its terrors. For what they knew was right they fought down the blitz; and hundreds of thousands of them bore the loss of homes and material possessions, of life and limb. Since then they have faced shock and boredom; crisis and disappointment; and they have kept their nerve, their courage and their devotion.

Now we can look forward to the days of victory—provided we do not regard it as easy or "just round the corner"—and our minds begin to turn to the question of what sort of nation we hope to make after the war. I ask nothing better for Britain than that she should face the problems of her own and the world's future in the same spirit in which she has faced the storms of war—putting first things first, and spirit above matter.

Lately we have all been thinking about a great post-war plan—the Beveridge Plan for social security. Of the Government's attitude to that particular plan I have at present nothing to say. But of the Government's intention to bring about a more secure standard of life for our people, many utterances by Ministers have already given proof. For myself I have no doubt that it is the duty of this, or any other Government, to make provision for a minimum standard of life that will keep our population, without exception, decently fed, and properly looked after in illness, misfortune and old age.

It may be asked, can we afford to do this?

I would say—can we afford *not* to do it? The mere instinct of self-preservation warns us not to allow in our midst the continued existence of a depressed, insufficiently fed minority. But if it did

[1] Delivered at Swindon, 20 December 1942.

not, the instincts of common humanity would prompt us not to leave our brothers and sisters in fear and in need, while our national family has the means to lift them up to decent living.

Once a community has reached a point of enlightenment and education where it is aware of the plight of its old, sick, out of work and unfortunate citizens, there is an imperative moral obligation upon it to care for them. This must be done. I myself see no practical reason, economic or financial, why it should not be done. I also feel that a cautious, niggling worldly wisdom, counting chances while children went hungry, would be a miserable foundation for our future life together as a family, and for that moral leadership which I trust Britain will long continue to give to the world.

But now, what is a social security scheme, after all? Don't let us get it out of focus. At best, it is nothing more than ambulance and salvage work: rescuing and patching up our social casualties: making good, so far as we can, the results of our failures in self-government. These things must be done; but the right basis to start from is that there shouldn't *be* any standing army of unemployed, any sick of preventable disease, any elderly people decrepit and infirm before the allotted span. In our true policy for the future, social security can play but a part and, if we succeed, it will and should be an ever-lessening part. We cannot rouse ourselves and others to heights of achievement with the slogan—minimum subsistence for all. We've got to provide it, but not regard it as an end in itself.

If we make it our ideal, and let it hypnotise us, not only shall we relapse into fatty degeneration of the spirit, but we shall find that by one means or another we have lost even the security at which we aimed so exclusively. Security is like happiness, as many an individual has found: if you put it first and make it your aim, you lose it. Security is like peace, as many a country has found: if you make it the isolated object of policy, you lose it.

I think it is this truth which is at the back of the minds of those who fear that schemes of social security may sap the people's initiative and enterprise and rob them of their will to work. They see the need of a spirit of effort, initiative and adventure, and I agree with them. I agree that if people have security and no purpose, no sense of loyalty to something beyond themselves, they will relapse into inertia. I agree that there are dangers in security alone. I remember that in the twenty years between the two wars, though we had too little social security, we had more of it in Britain than ever before, and yet we very nearly went to sleep and lost our freedom. But the conclusion I draw is different from that of the critics. I don't believe in the moral value of imposing security on people for its own sake. I don't believe in trying to whip them into achievement with the lash of fear and of want. I believe in getting the best out of people: I believe the best in our people is magnificently good: I believe they can be led to rise to great occasions in peace as in war: I believe that education is a better task-master than unemployment, leadership than want, faith than fear.

As we look forward to a world after the war, we can perceive a need for all that this country and this people can achieve of leadership and faith. It is not my purpose to-day to speak of international affairs, but on the Home Front there are points I should like to make.

Once again I turn to the hours of crisis for a reminder of what qualities we shall need in the post-war world. At that time one found a strong sense of national unity and a disregard of private and sectional interest—both of them based, not merely on the knowledge that our own lives were at stake but also, I am convinced, on the knowledge that the cause of all mankind had for that hour been entrusted to our keeping. There were many men and women for whom the bombs blasted away, not only bricks and mortar and all the trappings of their past lives, but also, for a time at least, the mistaken idea that these things really mattered, when weighed in the balance against that for which we stood—the hope of progress, the supremacy of law and truth, the dignity and fellowship of man.

After the war, the fate of our people will depend upon their power to put first things first. If I speak to-day of the national business of getting a living, it is not because I think that material standards are the most important, but because in this phase of man's history it is in the economic sphere that many of the most urgent and testing of his problems must be faced. We must rise above domination by our economic machine: cease to be the creatures of our own needs: be the masters, not the slaves, of material things. Our people have a right to be well fed and shod and housed and schooled: they have a right to achieve these things for themselves and to enjoy a sense of constructive usefulness in doing so. Not all their jobs can be inherently attractive, but all can be done with a sense of worthwhile purpose, as our jobs, whether dull or exciting in themselves, are done in war time.

Our economic life must be organised directly to achieve its object, a right standard of public well-being. That means turning our backs for ever on schemes of restriction, whether of goods or of labour. If, tempted by any short-term argument, we ever again dabble in such schemes, in that instant our national future is threatened and our scheme of social security becomes a burden instead of a benefit, a load on our shoulders instead of a weight off our minds. Never again dare we, on any grounds, whether economic or moral, be indifferent if our productive machine is standing idle or running down or if the energies of the people are unused or under-used. It will be suicidal, after the war, for financial authorities and Governments to stand by, while great industries are more than half idle and great areas of the country are in distress. We shall be unable to afford such folly. You may say we never could; and I agree. But in future we shall be brought sharply up against the fact that we can't afford it, and thereby led to ensure that it doesn't happen. This end will not be realised in a day. It will take discipline and patient struggle. But achieved it must and will be.

In my view to ensure full national output and a proper welfare standard for all, much of the social control of production which we have learnt to accept and to value during the war will need to be continued during the peace. And do not misunderstand this word "control". We have not adopted war-time public control for control's sake, or only to keep naughty producers in order. We have adopted it because of the paramount need to put the interest of the whole community first and because it is the best way of getting the most of what we want. People used to talk as though control were a cramping, limiting thing. It isn't. Wise social control is a stimulating, enlarging thing. I myself can see no sharp distinction in nature between the economic problems of war and the problems of the strenuous, difficult peace that lies before us. If control is right and useful to-day, nobody can assume it will be wrong and dangerous to-morrow.

Remember that enterprise doesn't have to be private in order to be enterprise. In the nineteenth century it might have been true to contrast the vigour and freshness of private enterprise with the restrictive effect of public regulations. In the twentieth century, with its inevitable trend towards centralised organisation of big industry, private control has often tended towards a slowing down of men's hands and of their minds, while many of the most remarkable examples of enterprise which the world can show have been public—from Britain's Electricity Grid to America's T.V.A. and Russia's Dnieper Dam.

Social control of production, however, may take many different forms; how much of it we want, and in what forms, cannot be settled in terms of any political dogma. The sole test must be whether the public interest is served by such measures in particular cases or not. Some forms of economic activity would, like our postal and telegraphic communications, respond well to ownership and management by a Department of State. But the public concern in this form is certainly not a universal panacea. Rather it is likely to be exceptional. What, for instance, should we do with our natural monopolies: industries which cannot be carried on properly at all except on a monopoly basis? It may be that instead of leaving them in private hands, tied down and hedged about by a tangle of statutory restrictions or bureaucratic checks, we should get better national service from them if we turned them into public corporations like the Central Electricity Board, the London Transport Board or, in another sphere, the B.B.C.

Again, what should be done with industries which are not natural monopolies but have, by their growth and development in modern conditions, come nearer and nearer to being monopolies in fact, through the operation of mergings and trade agreements or cartels, like the iron and steel or chemical industries? These are great basic industries on which national well-being in peace, and safety in war, directly depend. We can't leave them alone in their monopolistic glory—we don't want to turn Britain into a corporative state and to adopt Fascism in its economic form. The answer may be anything from a public corporation to some form of management under a board of directors with a nationally nominated chairman. The thing that matters is to secure in these large-scale basic industries a due measure of public guidance and public accountability—and these are not things which can be left to chance.

Then there are kinds of business where individual enterprise has a lot of value even in modern conditions—small businesses and some kinds of medium and small-scale manufacture. Here the answer may be that the community will best serve itself by standing aside, apart from insisting upon proper business practice and standard minimum pay and conditions for employees of all grades.

There will be a substantial place, too, as there is now, for the Co-operative Movement in trade, and also, I believe, for co-operative enterprise in agricultural production and marketing. Farmers may find the answer to many of their problems, and the means of preserving much of what is best in war-time arrangements, by schemes of mutual aid on a systematic basis.

After the war we shall, as a community, have to set about making the best living we can. We shall have to approach all our economic problems on the basis that the interest of the community comes first. We should, I believe, have an annual economic and industrial budget as we now have an annual financial budget. We shall need each year a statement of the cost, not merely of government, the social services and the armed forces, but also of our national needs for wages and salaries, new capital outlay and capital repairs and renewals. We shall, in fact, have to estimate the size, not merely as we do now, of the State budget, but of the national income as a whole, and relate it to the demands we want to make upon it. If it falls short, we shall have to find ways of increasing it; or else we shall have to reduce our demands on it and to decide where, in the national interest, the cuts must be made. After the war, successful government will need a basis of public statistics, much more extensive and far-reaching in kind than anything we possess to-day. No longer must we be in any doubt about whether we can afford this form of social security or that enlargement of government activity. Such questions must not be left to the conjectures of partisans with an axe to grind. They must be matters much more of ascertainable fact than they were before the war.

And now I come back to my starting-point. To adopt sound measures of law and administration is not enough. Our public policy as a whole will not be sound unless it is founded firmly upon a clear appreciation of values other than material ones. Efficient organisation of industry is right, but it is not enough. Social security, too, can be abused—at both ends of the economic scale. Poor people may learn to depend upon public schemes of welfare without developing a corresponding sense of their duty to the community. Richer people may equally defraud the community's productive labour force by enjoying their incomes without feeling or discharging a corresponding obligation.

We must be humane and understanding in our approach to such questions, but we must not be soft or sentimental. We want better standards than the old Victorian code of doing the best one can for oneself. We need to love our neighbour as ourselves, not merely in the sanctity of the home or in the circle of friends, but in the practical workaday world of business; and while one cannot enforce the golden rule by a process of law, one can build an economic society in which it is easier to be unselfish, and much less profitable to be selfish, than the world in which you and I grew up.

II

THE BRITISH COMMONWEALTH[1]

RECENTLY I spoke of post-war home policy and planning for welfare and security in Britain. But it would be a most pernicious fallacy to think that any plans and policies we adopted at home could secure the prosperity of our people unless means had been found to achieve the two great aims which must govern and dominate world policy after the war—universal security and universal prosperity.

World-wide peace and world-wide prosperity are elementary British interests. Let us ask ourselves what contributions of experience, of wisdom, of moral and political judgment we, the self-governing peoples of the British Commonwealth, can make to these ends. I have declared more than once recently—it is a fundamental point—that the record of the British people in this war, the manner in which they entered, have fought and are fighting it, shows that they still possess in the fullest measure those qualities of tough, practical idealism which have been the basis of their contribution to human progress. They have something to give which the world certainly needs. Their duty is to go on being true to the best in themselves for the world's benefit as well as their own.

I want the British Commonwealth to last—not just because it is British, but because it is good, and will be better yet. Without it, the world would lose a great factor of stability and progress, just when those things will be most needed.

That part of the Empire which is composed of the self-governing Dominions, the free association of democratic communities, in a manner never before or elsewhere seen, is a living proof that the typical British contribution to political progress is one which the nations cannot do without. The growth of that association is a model for a world long afflicted by problems arising from the

1 Delivered at Newcastle-on-Tyne, 10 January 1943.

unequal development of different lands and peoples. Every Dominion began as a dependency, annexed by settlement or con-quered by the sword. Most of them contain conquered minorities of other nationalities or races. Every one achieved full self-government by the practical working out of democratic principles, expressed in the demand and capacity for self-government in the dependency, and the willingness to grant it freely and fully in the Mother Country. And remember that the principle of growth is still active, the boundary between Dominions and dependencies is not fixed, and the trend is always towards freedom.

It is not enough for our friends or critics abroad to pay lip-service to the self-governing Commonwealth—it is necessary that they understand it. I am told that it is not everywhere understood that the self-governing Dominions are in fact, as well as in form, absolute masters of their own political destinies. Everyone knows that there is common allegiance to The King, who is the head of the family and who symbolises so effectively the common ideas and aims which are the real bond between the Dominions. But the fact remains that each is perfectly free, without limit or reserva-tion. I can understand that other peoples may rub their eyes at this spectacle of a family of adult nations, each member with its own environment, problems and interests, freely moving and acting together in matters of life and death importance. Surely there must be a catch in it somewhere! Well, there is no catch. The freedom and independence are real. And the proof is in Eire, which decided to stay out of the war and was left free to do so, to the great hurt of the Empire's cause and with little advantage to her reputation. We take all this for granted—others might well ponder over it. When they do genuinely comprehend the moral and political achievement which it represents they will be in a better position to pronounce upon the qualities and the value of that part of the Empire which is still dependent in status.

Turn now to that other part, India and the colonies, graded in political development all the way from some primitive community in the early stages of tutelage up to Ceylon, which has so much of the substance of self-government, and to India, which, after the war, can have full self-government for the taking. We know that one of the main motives for the acquisition of many of these colonial territories was commercial. Commercial interest still plays a part, not always beneficent, in their affairs. But from an early stage, this original motive was, so far as official policy was concerned, influenced to an increasing extent by quite a different one—a motive of duty, a sense of a job to be done for the people whom we found in our care, and for the sake of our own self-respect. The colonial record has had blots and blemishes. The picture to-day is far from perfect. But no one can explain the progress that has taken place since the commencement of the British connection— progress in public order, health, income, education, social services and the seeds of citizenship—except by recognising the operation of motives and policies quite other than commercial.

I would credit us also with laying the foundations of a good system of law and public administration. On the whole, and with some exceptions, I would credit us with a humane, decent, fair-minded attitude towards the less advanced peoples in our charge. In these matters we have set an example which the enlightened world has been glad to follow. Established British policy was in a way the model taken by the League of Nations in the first flush of its youthful idealism. I would draw comfort from one fact of recent history. In the weeks after Dunkirk, when there was scarcely a dependency in the world that could not have got free of the British connection if it had been bursting with the desire to do so, the great majority gave tangible proof of the most touching loyalty to the British connection.

We are no greedy exploiters. I am quite sure that your really scientific exploiter would be (indeed in his Nazi, Japanese and other forms he is) filled with scorn for our shortcomings in this regard. The British Government puts a lot of money each year into the Colonies and seeks no commercial return. The home country has rejected all temptation to be a monopolist. In peace-time it was selling the Colonies only about a quarter of the goods they bought and made no difficulty about their sending elsewhere nearly two-thirds of what they themselves produced. The British importer bought from the colonies only 8 per cent of what he required. The British investor put more money into Europe than into the whole of the colonies—more money into the Dutch East Indies than into the whole of British Africa. In peace-time the great rubber plantations of Ceylon send most of their products to America. Malaya sent four times as much of her wealth of rubber and tin to America as to Britain. If other great countries in more than one continent had been as liberal in their trading policies, as free from taint of aggressive economics, as was Great Britain with her colonies, the creeping paralysis of restriction and decline might not have set in, contributing as it did to war.

I could, however, wish that our constructive social and economic policies had matched the political enlightenment and humane integrity of our colonial administration. That there has been material progress from which native populations have benefited I am well aware: but, until recently at any rate, there has not been enough drive, system and urgency about our attempts to organise the economic life and better the livelihood of colonial peoples. For this defect public opinion at home must bear its share of responsibility. People haven't been interested enough in the colonies: everyone has meant well by them, but many people have wanted them looked after without having to bother too much about them. If we want constructive policies and progressive purposes in colonial government we can't expect them to grow spontaneously out of administrations on the spot. They must be *our* policies and *our* purposes, clearly understood and genuinely felt.

I want, therefore, to see the adoption in a still fuller and more practical spirit of the principle of administering the colonies positively for the benefit of their own people. In the long-term sense, the interests of colonial peoples are in line, broadly speaking, with those of the rest of the world. But if there is a conflict of short-term interest, for instance between the needs of the world for more raw materials, and the needs of colonial peoples to grow more food for themselves, then their need must come first without question. And their need for help in management, industrial and agricultural technique, and up-to-date methods of distribution and marketing should be met by the operation of Development Boards or other economic agencies under some suitable form of public control. Nowhere in the world is there a stronger case for the enlightened work of such public economic instrumentalities ·than in the colonies. Private undertakings are responsible to no one but their shareholders, and we should not have on our consciences the irresponsible handling by powerful bodies of the economic destinies of these partially developed peoples. We do not need as a country to approach our task in any quixotic spirit: fertile trade between peoples is beneficial to all concerned. This is as true of trade with colonial peoples as with anyone else, and we, all of us, have full right to the benefits of our share in the partnership. But our colonial trust, if we really regard it as a trust, has to be discharged in a responsible spirit of public duty, and with no vexatious conflicts between public policy and private interest.

We must, too, be ready to spend more freely to set the colonies economically on their feet. Here, too, I do not advocate impractical spendthrift policies, but a casting of our bread upon the waters, even if it returns to us only after many days, and then not in the form of exclusive markets or of large dividends, but of those other, far more valid rewards—the growth of contented progressive communities, good neighbours, and valued economic partners, whose progress serves not only themselves, but us and the rest of the world.

There must go with this policy of economic development a policy of labour advancement and of enabling undeveloped and partially developed communities to get practical training in political arts and governmental capacity. It would be sheer nonsense—ignorant, dangerous nonsense—to talk about grants of full self-government to many of the dependent territories for some time to come. In those instances it would be like giving a child of ten a latch-key, a bank account and a shot-gun. But we can combine forward policies of education with opportunities for the native peoples to take a developing part in forms of self-government appropriate to their own circumstances. Britons themselves have found the parish pump a fine training school for democracy.

I hope that after the war we shall find it possible to achieve, without prejudice to our own primary obligation for the well-being and progress of British territories, some wider pooling of tasks and responsibilities with others—always assuming that when it comes to the point there turn out to be others who are as ready to accept responsibility as to offer advice, as ready to share burdens as benefits.

But this is only one example of the fact that after the war the whole British Commonwealth—not the colonies alone—will need to, and will want to, adopt as a condition of its own survival, enlightened policies of international co-operation, and that if it were so foolish as to think otherwise it would be sealing its own doom. After the war, no Power, however great, will be able single-handed to ensure its own security. If the Empire were to try it would cripple itself in the attempt, and I doubt if it could succeed. There will be few regions of the globe where Britain, the Dominions and colonies will not have, as near and interested neighbours, Great Powers, each at least as powerful in its own part of the world as the British Commonwealth could possibly hope to be in that arena. Only in a wider system of political security will the Commonwealth find its own salvation: and its nature as a world-wide society means that no more limited system can service its needs.

Again, the peoples of the Commonwealth will be quite unable to work out policies of economic welfare for themselves on the basis of an exclusive cultivation of their own imperial garden. The countries of the Commonwealth need the rest of the world, just as it needs them, as a market and a source of supplies. Without it they would be a poor and limited society, for all their own wealth. The myth of a self-sufficient Empire has gone the way of other historical illusions, and I hope and believe that British commonsense has said goodbye to it for ever.

Before the war many of the wisest and most far-seeing of British patriots—the Prime Minister himself most notable among them—had the sagacity to see that the prosperity and the success of the League of Nations was a primary British interest, and that its failure was a lamentable British defeat. In just the same way we who believe in the British Commonwealth and will be working for its continued life and usefulness will for that very reason be thinking on terms of still wider partnerships, political and economic.

One of the most idealistic of American statesmen, Mr Henry Wallace, recently remarked that every foreign policy must have in it a strain of self-interest. That is profoundly true. It is the duty of peoples to care for themselves and of their governments to care for them. Political quixotism is meaningless—it could not succeed, not even in winning the confidence of other nations. We need not therefore apologise for proclaiming that enlightened world co-operation in the political and economic sphere is an essential British interest. Rather can we say that one of the strongest claims of the British system on the confidence of other nations, great and small, is that the long-term interests of our Empire are wholly in accord with the long-term interests of the international society of nations as a whole. Of that international society I shall hope to speak on some other occasion. To-day, I am content if I have reminded you of the first charge upon our thought and energies—our own Empire—and how that charge leads us inescapably on to world citizenship. That is in our best tradition.

III

THE FUTURE OF EXPORTS[1]

SHALL we be richer or poorer after the war?

You remember how the aftermath of war was coped with last time. The people of Britain and their rulers were so heartily sick of war conditions that they wanted nothing but to be rid of everything to do with the war. War had been a time of rather slowly developing rationing and controls. "Very well," we said, "let us get rid of rationing and controls. Let us have supply and demand. Let people spend the accumulated savings of the war as they will, let industry loose to meet their impatient demands as best it can."

Well, it looked very nice for a time. Savings were spent, prices rose, goods were turned out, people got jobs and there was a fine old boom—for about 18 months. At the end of that time the country had a bad slump, lasting another 18 months in its extreme form, and lasting to some degree for many years. I remember that one of my first jobs as Mayor of Hackney in 1920–21 was to organise an unemployment relief fund, and another was, with other people, to call on the Prime Minister (Mr Lloyd George) in Scotland and worry him about schemes of work. He responded energetically, but there had not been worked out in advance any well thought-out policy, there was no real plan, and so unemployment stayed with us for a long, long time. Those first three or four post-war years were a sad, mad, silly time, both in economics and in other walks of life, and I profoundly hope they will never be repeated.

This time, we want to switch over from war economy to peace economy as quickly as we can, but sensibly, knowing what we are doing, and without a hang-over, without a morning after the night before.

[1] Delivered at the Annual Meeting of the East Midland Regional Conference of the Labour Party, Nottingham, 13 February 1943.

In short, we must have rationing in appropriate forms for the sake of fairness at home, and for the sake of keeping the ship of State on an even keel. We must have raw material controls too because it will be as necessary then as it is now to make certain that first things come first, that our export trade gets what it needs and that at home the various commodities go where they will do most good in getting back to a sound peace basis. We shall also want price control, without which there would certainly be astronomical rises in price with all the dangers of inflation at a time when everyone will be rushing to buy and we shall be suffering severely from war-time shortages.

Quite recently the Chancellor of the Exchequer (Sir Kingsley Wood), in his notable speech in the House of Commons, has told the country clearly that this is the policy which we must adopt after the war. I am certain it will be accepted. We have managed our war-time rationing and controls infinitely better than last time—it is quite reasonable to expect that we shall show a very much improved record after the war as well.

Moreover, we shall have good prospects to look forward to. The progress of scientific knowledge is always going on. Very likely, as a result of the tremendous boost which war gives to scientific work, it will go on afterwards more rapidly than ever. We shall have new substances to work with, new industries growing up to handle them. We shall find Nature more submissive to man's will than ever before in human history.

We have certainly learned some of the lessons of past mistakes; we have learned much better how to make our money system our servant instead of the cruel task-master which has exacted so many unnecessary sacrifices from us in the past. We aren't likely to let a deflationary financial policy throttle our constructive energies in the interest of some mystical mumbo-jumbo about pre-war exchange parities or gold values. We have learned a great deal about how to control unemployment—at least I am hopeful that we have learned. Certainly there is now a great measure—a surprising measure—of agreement among economists and experts of many different schools about the steps which the State can take to avoid the extremes of boom and slump and to keep within manageable bounds the volume of unemployment. In short, we have at our hand all the technical means to ensure prosperity. We shall know enough to be able to work and plan for more production, and when we get it to make it yield a higher standard of living, instead of yielding for millions of people only unemployment and want. If we can deal firmly with the forces of selfishness and sectionalism, wherever they are found, which seek for their own narrow and misguided purposes to come between us and our future, we can look to that future full of hope.

But of course when we look beyond our own borders, the issue is not solely in our hands. Yet the international economic issue is one upon which our own fate and future entirely depend. When we look to the future we must get accustomed to certain simple, fundamental facts. I will set them out like a kindergarten lesson. Indeed, that is what they are, our kindergarten lesson in post-war foreign trade.

First, if we want to keep up our standard of life, let alone to increase it, we shall have to go on importing, on much the same scale as before, although we must make up our minds to keep our home agricultural production at as high a level as is consistent with sound economic practice.

Secondly, we shall have much less interest from foreign investments because most of those investments will have been realised to beat Hitler, and we shall have to reconstruct them.

Thirdly, it is doubtful whether our shipping and financial services will bring us in the income they did—we certainly cannot count upon it.

Fourthly and last; it therefore follows that we shall have to increase our export of goods, probably by several hundreds of millions of pounds—and it isn't too soon to be aware of the problem and to apply our minds to its solution.

The old way of tackling it would be to say: "There is only so much world trade to be done, and if the other fellow gets our share we shall have to go without. So let us fight, let us make arrangements to keep the other fellow out of as many markets as we can; let us cut our prices, and cut his throat, in the markets where we do have to face him. And if a country isn't buying from us as much as we think it ought to, let us refuse to buy its goods. Then it will be poorer still and will buy still less, whether from us or from anybody else."

I do not wish to stir up old controversies about Free Trade *v.* Protection; there was perhaps a fair amount of unreality about both sides of that argument.

But I do say that that old method, the method of Beggar-my-Neighbour, is wrong and doomed to failure, as it has always failed. It is economic war, no matter how polite the names we give it. It will lead, as it always has led, to military war.

It is based on the utterly false assumption that there is a fixed amount of world trade to be done, and that, if somebody else does it, we won't. The truth is that there lies before all nations the possibility of a tremendous expansion in world trade, as in industry at home. Industrial growth has taken place in many countries overseas. This is fine for us—don't think of it as making competitors, think of it as making markets. If we pin our faith too exclusively to our export industries in their old forms, built up to supply the needs of backward countries, we shall suffer as other countries become richer and less backward. But if we are ready to take care of the newer needs of industrially developing countries, if we are lively in our thinking and planning, our making and selling, then every increase in the riches of China or India or our own colonies, or anywhere else, can add to our own export opportunities and our own prosperity.

This presents to us in Britain the task of ensuring that our export industries are as efficient and active as possible. Personal enterprise built up these industries in the very different circumstances of the past, but after the war that initiative will need to be supported and indeed I would say guided by the State.

I always try to approach such questions, not in the light of preconceived dogmas but in the light of genuine national interest. I am quite satisfied that the State has the absolute right to take a strong and useful hand in the solution of the export problem, because it affects the vital welfare of the nation and its standard of life. The State, at the very least, must set the targets and ensure that nothing is left undone to reach them. I was glad to hear the President of the Board of Trade (Mr Hugh Dalton) tell Parliament last week, in his lively and stimulating speech, how export industry and the State are beginning to get together now to plan for efficiency.

In my opinion we shall need to broaden the whole conception of public policy in relation to the export trades after the war—we shall need to work upon the basis of a much closer partnership between the State and industry in which each has rights but each also has important obligations to the other. My own programme for export could be summed up under five headings.

To begin with, a factual examination, industry by industry, of resources and weaknesses, assets and difficulties, potential foreign markets and the means to serve them.

Secondly, a greatly improved consular service equipped with the means not only to analyse markets abroad for the information of industry at home, but ready also to work in close and constructive collaboration with the representatives of our industries and their customers on the spot. Some of the changes announced in the recent Foreign Office White Paper point in this direction.

Thirdly, an extensive programme of commercial and technical education, carried out under the stimulus and supervision of the State, aiming to raise to new levels the quality of recruits who will come forward for the work of research, management, production and marketing.

Fourthly, a right on the part of the State to examine the situation and circumstances of any export industry which is in difficulties or not showing satisfactory results or in need of help, either in its own estimation or in the estimation of the Government; and a readiness on the part of the State to give help in meeting the need whatever it is, whether capital re-equipment or a better standard of labour—provided that the home market, equally with the export markets, shall benefit from such friendly help and that the State shall have the means to satisfy itself that the help is used in the national interest.

Fifthly, the relation thus envisaged between the State and industry should be a partnership, a two-way affair, in which each party has something to teach the other. To that end we shall need large elements in the Civil Service trained not exclusively in administration but in the methods and outlook of industry and commerce, so that they can work harmoniously with the business world and be regarded by it not as interfering busybodies but as friends and helpers. Such a system of partnership with due recognition of mutual obligation would avoid the errors of unbridled individualism or restrictive monopoly on the one hand, and of burdensome, interfering bureaucracy on the other. Whatever later developments may be, this seems a fair and practical solution to a pressing national problem.

If one looked only at the record of our export industries in the period between the wars one might well be a little disheartened about future prospects. But look at the proud and remarkable achievement of our industrial system in this war, an achievement not surpassed by any country under any system—one to which our enemies themselves point as an example. Consider the remarkable result of this war-time partnership of the State and industry. See how, with all its imperfections—and nothing human is perfect—it has helped to release the brains and energies, the ingenuity and inventiveness and drive of our people. Are not there lessons here for the critical post-war years?

Looking forward then past the necessary stringencies and shortages of the earlier post-war years, I see the hope of a bright future for Britain and the world—a future, however, that is shadowed by two great question marks.

One is the problem of our population—our decline in birth-rate. It is coming to be generally realised that if we are to maintain our population anywhere near its present level we must be able to count upon a considerable increase in the size of the average family. Some experts have calculated that to keep a population of 42 millions, that is four millions less than our present population, we should need to have families on the average 25 per cent bigger than those of to-day—a very big increase. The task of building a social order that will induce such an increase in the birth-rate provides one of the greatest tests of the wisdom and foresight of our people and the statesmanship of our leaders. It is no use talking alone about the selfishness and laziness of parents. There may be something in that, but it is open to doubt whether parents are more selfish and lazier now than they have ever been; on the whole they think more about their children's welfare. But they have got new ideas and standards, both for themselves and for their children. They are increasingly refusing to have families if this is going to mean that the children are ill-fed, ill-cared for or poorly educated, or that the mother must become a perpetual drudge, ruining her life and health. In any case we have to face it, so we had better set to work to provide the right answer. It is time to work out a national charter of childhood, and a charter of motherhood, setting up standards that will satisfy the reasonable aspirations of parents for their children and themselves. We must bear in mind the fact that until people feel happy about having more children, and want to have more, patriotic appeals will get us nowhere.

That then is the first question mark to which it will be our task to find the right answer.

The second takes us beyond our own borders to that world of international economic relations of which I have already spoken. We must face the fact that both at home and abroad the old economic ideas are still very strong.

It is an unhappy fact—we saw it demonstrated after the last war —that newly liberated nations have a tendency towards extreme, sometimes even aggressive economic nationalism. It is perhaps a natural reaction from the suppression of nationalism from which they have suffered. But it is a danger to them and to the world. Other nations, too, nations which have not this excuse (and I am not excepting anybody, including ourselves), find it easy to slip into the old rut of economic nationalism, separatism, isolationism, and the aggressive grabbing for markets and profits.

Yet it is as certain as daylight that at the end of the old road of economic nationalism there lies one more bitter, bloody lesson for humanity, prefaced by one more period of poverty and depression where there could be enrichment and prosperity. International trade on a nationalist, competitive basis is economic war; economic war leads to military war; attempts at economic domination will be resisted like attempts at military domination, and will divide the world into warring camps.

So the question is, are we going to set out towards hope or towards despair? Both at home and abroad that issue is before us. We cannot alone lay down economic policies for the world, but we can give the right lead—or hasten to follow if it is given elsewhere.

I ask nothing more of Britain than that she should face and deal with the problems of the post-war world in the spirit of 1940. That is no mere rhetorical turn of phrase. For what was the spirit of 1940? It was not the spirit which said: "The Germans have the guns, the troops, the planes; our allies are struck down; we have no tanks or artillery. We must be prudent; we must face the facts; we must avoid Utopian idealism and wishful thinking. Arithmetic is too much for us. We must surrender." That, happily, was not the spirit of 1940. The British spirit of 1940 was the fine, brave spirit of Winston Churchill who declared, in that menacing situation, "we shall fight on the beaches......we shall fight in the streets......we shall never surrender". Let that be the spirit in which we face the economic problems of the post-war world. Let us not say, "our imports are high; our exports are low; our wealth is reduced; we cannot expect to change the world; we must be prudent; arithmetic is too much for us; we must surrender—reduce our standard of living, turn our backs on social progress, cut our wages, and try to keep our heads above water by treading the other fellow down".

Let us rather say in the true spirit of 1940 that we know and understand the right course to pursue—the course of courage and enlightened foresight; that we intend to strike out upon a path of glorious and constructive adventure with every ounce of our strength and determination, trusting that the rightness and wisdom of our policy, and the conviction bred of our example, will raise up companions in courage and wisdom by our side.

IV

WORLD POLITICS[1]

THERE are two separate ways of approaching the question of the post-war organisation of the world, and they each of them lead to the same destination.

One is political and springs from a consideration of the fundamental question of security. How do we plan to safeguard international peace in the future? Obviously the immediate post-war task is to disarm the aggressor nations, and to put it beyond possibility that they can trouble the peace of the world again until enough time has elapsed for a genuine and deep change of heart and mind among their misguided and deluded peoples. It is natural and right to look forward to a period in which the victorious Allies, the United Nations, will constitute themselves the guardians of world peace. Among the United Nations a special responsibility rests upon the Great Powers, particularly on Russia, the United States, China and ourselves, as wielders of what will be the overwhelming preponderance of armed might in the world. The sword of world justice and world sovereignty will be in the hands of these four nations. What the next stage will be is shown by the history of every politically developed country of the world. First you have the forging, whether by slow development or quick military action, of the sword of power. Then comes the problem of backing power with consent, of securing a firm political basis for the necessary engine of government or control. That will be the world's problem too. The four Great Powers must see to it that in course of time they mobilise, behind the effective power they will wield, the free consent of all the free peoples of the world, including the politically reconstituted nations who have been victims of the Axis. Without that the sword, however mighty its blade and keen its edge, will soften or splinter in their hands.

[1] Delivered at the Guildhall, City of London, 24 February 1943.

This points towards the creation in due time of a genuinely representative world political association. I do not attempt to give it a name, for names may raise memories or rouse prejudices. This association must provide the means by which the peoples of the world will find the necessary solutions for world problems. No more must such solutions be sought by an unregulated and precarious balance of power or by the perilous bargainings of separate armed nations. It must be sought by reasoned and moderate joint approaches to questions of difficulty and problems of change— approaches in which there is general readiness to sacrifice the old idea of unrestricted national sovereignty, in the interest of common action.

If that is a Utopian ideal, then the hope of world peace is an illusory hope, for only by this means can that hope be realised. Nor is this Utopia—if it be Utopia—a private dream of my own. His Majesty's Government must all be Utopians. They have committed themselves, through the mouth of the Foreign Secretary in a fine Parliamentary speech last December—nothing like as well known as it should be—to precisely this objective. A world association is the aim; fully representative (as the League of Nations was not) with a unified resolve to work out and implement a positive policy (such as the League of Nations had not) and possessing (as the League did not) a force fully sufficient to achieve its agreed purposes and to restrain those who would impede them.

But incidentally remember that this does not necessarily mean a very great force. We hear a good deal of an international police force, mentioned as though it meant the occupation by military forces of all the dangerous or strategically significant parts of the world for all time. A police force means no such thing: it means a civil agency of inspection, supervision and control, with a military force in the background that need only be of moderate size, though sufficient for the purpose, because it has no competing military forces to reckon with. We need not, thank heaven, look forward to the indefinite maintenance of heavy arms burdens after the clean-up period, always provided—and this brings us back to the starting-point—that the crucial problems of world organisation have been solved, and that aggressive nations—such as Germany—are not permitted even the beginnings of dangerous re-armament. We must not be lazy or slack about this. We and the other United Nations must be ready at all times to jump, by military action if need be, on any potential aggressor directly he *begins* to prepare. There must be no sloppiness about it—no waiting while the danger grows, as we did with the Nazis.

So much then for the approach from the point of view of security. The second great approach is by way of those concrete economic and social problems whose solution is as essential to the permanent success of a security policy as genuine security is to the world's progress.

The overriding need is to secure an expanding volume of production and trade-production within each nation, and trade between them. The problem is to take the necessary measures to bring this about and to remove the obstacles in the way of it.

One thing the world must not do: it must not surrender to economic and financial things as they are. It cannot ignore facts; it must be practical and sensible. But, no less, it has the duty wisely to direct the forces of production and to shape them to public ends.

Take a topical British example. In the House of Commons Debate on the Beveridge Report last Thursday I made two issues plain. To enter into large and growing financial commitments without a proper survey of public finances as a whole and taking due, but not timorous, account of other financial factors, would be madness. The British electorate, including the working-class electorate, will not stand for that. But in the same speech I also stressed—and I make it plain now in and to the City of London itself, a place that at times needs such a reminder—that we must not sit back and accept the national income, with its financial consequences, as it is. We have to be active in changing financial facts.

It is essential that steps be taken to increase the national production and income. Not only that, but to see to it that it is fairly and equitably distributed. We shall not get the best out of our people unless they know that more production, more effort, will bring a better standard of life as its reward. We have to get away from that abominable set of economic circumstances in which more production sometimes meant more unemployment, more effort meant more poverty. Poverty in the midst of—and at times because of—plenty has been a disgrace to us all. War has substantially ended that shame. It will be a scandal if peace starts it up again.

In short, as I have been urging for years past, "Man must become the Master and not the Slave of Material Things".

That doctrine should go for Britain. It should also go for the world. Let all mankind assert its dignity and mastery.

What then are the main first steps in international policy leading to that end?

In the sphere of world economic relationships let us look first at three great focal problems, three C's—Currency, Commodities, Commerce. We have to find a means of organising our monetary relationships that will foster an expanding world trade instead of emphasising the nationalist obstacles in its way. It must be stable without being rigid; it must enable credit balances to fertilise instead of freezing the world's resources. It must reflect the real weights in the international economic balance, without turning those weights into millstones round the necks of the nations. This may sound theoretical, but I believe there is enough general agreement among the world's economic and financial experts to secure, with a certain amount of give and take, an agreed solution.

The same is true, I am convinced, of the problem of finding means to avoid those catastrophic changes in the prices of the great basic foods and raw materials upon which world prosperity and the security of peoples so directly depend.

And thirdly, there is the problem of reconciling the concern which each country feels for the state of its own industry and the social balance of its own community, with the requirements of an expanding world economy and the overriding need to increase the wealth of all nations by a maximum exchange of their goods and services. Here too, I believe a practicable answer can be found in terms of international organisation and in a form—this is essential—which will enable centrally planned systems like the Russian, so called "liberal" systems, and mixtures of the two, all to participate effectively.

Though this is not the time to go into details, it is my conviction that the technical means of solving all these problems can be found and that what is required now is a determined application of the minds of the nations to the achievement of agreed solutions.

Then, in close association with the three C's, is the question of international control of investment so as to send the world's capital surpluses to the points where they will do most good. The places that are most backward and starved of capital are not always those which offer the readiest commercial return on investment. This is where international control, and I may add international self-control and long-term thinking, are required. This is one of the ways in which we shall give reality to the Atlantic Charter.

Then there are questions of international labour standards; international health standards and policies; and more important almost than any other, the elaboration of an international food and nutrition policy which, rightly developed, can itself be one of the most powerful of all forces in aid of an expanding world economy.

Some of these problems are upon us now; at least in the form of their war-time equivalents and precursors—problems of supply and raw material allocation, of relief and rehabilitation. Other problems, if they are not now actually upon us, can clearly be foreseen in their general post-war shape.

The more constructively and systematically we are thinking about these things in the governing centres of the United Nations, the more surely are we creating the very stuff and content of post-war international relationships.

So whether we approach the whole matter from the side of politics or from the side of economics and social affairs, we are led irresistibly to the same conclusion. We cannot make progress except in organised association. We cannot—none of the United Nations can—get on satisfactorily with its own affairs except by taking thought for the affairs of the rest. The impact upon the rest of the world of events in some countries may be greater, according to their size, their material resources, their human skill, their moral leadership. But it is true of all, of the smallest state as well as the greatest, that what they have to contribute counts greatly. That is true both positively and negatively. Each has the power to give, each also has the power to become an economic or social plague spot infecting the rest.

These questions cannot be left until the morrow of the armistice. Mr Eden in the speech to which I have referred makes it quite clear that this is the view of His Majesty's Government. And another spokesman, America's Under-Secretary of State for Foreign Affairs, has made the same point a few days earlier. He said:

"Another essential is the reaching of agreement between the United Nations before the armistice is signed upon those international adjustments which we believe to be desirable and necessary for the maintenance of a peaceful and prosperous world for the future."

We may have to look forward to some years of world-wide war yet. It may be—no one can prophesy either way—that European peace will come upon us comparatively soon. Do not, I beg of you, assume that. Too many are conducting themselves as if the war were all over, bar the shouting. But anyone who knows something of the history of Anglo-American co-operation in the field of supply will know that even under the most favourable auspices, with every door of mutual comprehension and communication wide open, it takes a long time to rub off all the corners, to learn all the mutual lessons and to shake down into a harmoniously working international unit. This limited and two-sided experience sharpens the lesson of the need for getting on with the many-sided job that waits in those even wider fields of which I have spoken.

And what shall be the role of Great Britain, herself, in this international association of nations? She has, I would suggest, three parts to play.

In the first place, of the Great Powers who will inevitably play the leading part in hammering out solutions to these problems, she is the oldest and politically the most experienced. I do not suggest that she has always used her experience to the full. What I do say is that she has the opportunity to draw once again, for the benefit of all the world, upon that fund of political sagacity and wisdom which has served her and other nations well in many crises of the past. She has had a longer experience in self-government than any country; she has had a wider experience of world government in all areas, among peoples of all levels of development, than any; she has enjoyed (and, oddly enough, in some respects I think that is the right word), she has enjoyed in this war a moral bath, and can approach the tasks of the peace with her instincts and her energies refreshed and renewed. Here is a quality, or skill, or genius—call it what you will—which created the first self-government (and I need not remind an audience in the City of London how far back that goes), which nourished the Mother of Parliaments, which has shown modern evidence of its continuing vitality in the creation of a world society of self-governing Dominions. Need we doubt that this power and this people can contribute a fund of moral authority, leadership and wisdom to the post-war councils of nations?

Secondly, the ties of geography—closer than ever in the days of the aeroplane—make us a part of Europe. So does the tradition of a common culture, in art, letters, music, architecture, in scientific theory and its application, and in many respects in politics too. Yet, by our membership of a world-wide Commonwealth and by the ties of common language and like institutions which bind us to the United States of America, we are inevitably far more than European. We must be a link between Europe and the world; in some respects perhaps an interpreter, for, with our sister nations of the Commonwealth, we may be able to explain the modes of thought, aspirations and policies of the new world to the old, and of the old world to the new. In particular, we may be able to play a part in developing and cementing relations of friendship between our two great allies—the Russians and Americans. They have already a great deal in common in those attributes of great size and large-scale industrial development which play so great a part in shaping the outlook of nations. But it may be that we shall find ourselves able to strengthen their mutual understanding, since we shall share with each of them problems and preoccupations which form no part of the direct experience of the other. With Russia we share a direct, first-hand concern with the crucial problems of reorganisation, development, and peace in Europe: with America, a sea-going, world-wide outlook.

Lastly, it is my conviction that we have a peculiar part to play in world development because of the fact that our interests are, in so many respects, world-wide, and thus identical with the interests of international understanding. Since her growth to the full stature of world power, Great Britain has been a foremost exponent and practitioner of those ideas and policies which have best served the cause of world solidarity. Whatever tells most powerfully in favour of peace on sea and land, of good understanding among the nations, of expanding commerce and greater political freedom, tells powerfully in favour of the interests of Britain and the British Commonwealth. Not for the first time, I emphasise the point that this is one of our greatest claims to a position among the leaders of the nations and to the confidence of our associates.

To be frank, I would add that in the period between the two wars—not the most glorious in our history—we tended to slip back from our own standards towards policies of separatism, sectionalism and a reluctance to assume the full responsibilities of world citizenship. In our defence I would only plead that we were by no means the first backsliders either in economics or politics; indeed, we might claim whatever share of credit may be due to those who formed the rearguard of that sorry procession of retreat and defeat which heralded the onset of war. But I hope that future generations will be able to look back upon that phase as just a tragically mistaken interlude, and that we shall, from now on, set our feet again upon a course of international policy which will range Great Britain as a powerful friend on the side of expansion, peace and progress in the world.

And so I leave my theme, having, I hope, shared with you the mood which I feel—a mood of reasoned optimism about the future of our people and of the world, but a mood also of eagerness to see us, with our allies, planning now the future world that we wish to see. These are the formative years. The sinister forces of chance and chaos must shape a future that will loom darkly over the lives of our children, unless we here and now begin to shape that future consciously, according to our vision.

V

THE STATE AND INDUSTRY[1]

I WANT to-day to talk over with you the present position and some of the problems facing the Labour Party. We must all of us feel some concern about the best way for the party to make that contribution to national greatness and world progress which we all feel instinctively it ought to make, and can make.

The progress of social reform in our country has owed far more to the Labour and Socialist Movement than can be measured by the legislative achievements of the party itself in those brief and baffled interludes when it has held office.

The party's entire history as an organised political force has been short. It has been much in opposition and little in office. Much of what it has effected has sprung from its presence as a leaven in the political lump, rather than from its own deliberate, responsible work as a Government. Moreover, it has sometimes been out-manœuvred by opponents. Once it was abandoned by leaders whom it had trusted and who fully shared with their party any responsibility for the difficulties which it encountered.

The effect of this, inevitably, has tended to reduce the party's self-confidence. In the last ten years its mood has perhaps created the impression that it does not accept responsibilities with ease, and that it tends to think in terms of "opposition". Does it not often overlook the value of the half loaf—or more—which it has won, and go into private and public mourning over the further half—or less—which on some particular occasion it has not won? We have not yet acquired the poise and self-assurance of "rulers". We are defeatist often instead of being fully conscious of our own influence and power.

1 Delivered at the Annual Meeting of the Yorkshire Regional Council of the Labour Party at Leeds, 3 April 1943.

What we want is a more confident, assured approach to our problems and tasks—a belief not only in the rightness of our cause but in the power of that right cause to win its way to victory. We have had our share of electoral defeats. Too many. No party can thrive on defeat. Psychologically and mentally we must condition ourselves for success and be ready for the tasks of government.

The party must have learned from the political history of the past twenty-five years that appeals for change made on grounds of sectional interest as such, whether from the Right or from the Left, do not win political consent or conviction in this country. The right and hopeful spirit in which to put our aims forward is the big, broad, crusading, idealistic spirit. Social idealism unites, sectionalism divides. If our approach is in terms of the good of the nation as a whole, the nation as a whole will respond to our lead and rally under our banner.

Labour must be more, in practice, than a party of social services and wage standards. It must hold up before this nation an ideal that will call forth the best in our people, an ideal of abundant life achieved by working together for common ends. And it must present this, not in the form of a stereotyped selection of planks from the traditional party platform, phrased in the somewhat special language we use among ourselves in the party conference room, but in the form of simple, clear proposals, up-to-date in their bearing upon current problems, and expressed in plain language which the ordinary citizen can at once understand.

Let me try to give a concrete example of what I mean. A fundamental question, as I reminded the House in the Beveridge Debate, is how the community is to get its living—the question of production, the question of the relation between the State and industry.

After the war we shall have to solve this problem in all of its three parts—how to get full employment, how to increase the productive efficiency of industry, and how to spread the increased product widely and fairly.

To approach these three tremendous questions from the point

of view of a preconceived dogma is not right, and also it is no use, because the country will neither understand nor listen. Neither the slogan of all-round nationalisation nor the slogan of all-round decontrol (even if one adds the saving clause "after the transitional period") are, as such, the slightest use to the country. The one general principle that has some meaning and can be defended is that the interest of the community and not the interest of this or that group in industry or elsewhere must decide these questions.

This brings me to my example. There is one crucial matter which affects all the three parts of the problem I have referred to—the matter of monopolies, their place in society, and the way in which society must deal with them.

One group of these monopolies are the so-called "natural" monopolies, like Gas, Electricity and (in effect) Transport, which are also, like Coal, common service industries and, like it, are ripe —or over-ripe—for public ownership and management. Another group consists of fully-fledged trusts, of most of which the same thing might be said. But to-day I want to deal more fully with monopolies of another and very important kind, presenting all the characteristic dangers and evils without necessarily being in an appropriate state for full public ownership in the early post-war period.

I refer to the great assortment of cartels, price rings, federations, price-fixing combines and so forth. Monopolies they are, in the sense that they have monopolised the control of their industry and its market and are in a position to impose their terms of trade on their customers and the community. While there is, of course, a place for the legitimate trade association, so long as it is not restrictive in spirit and tendency, many of these other organisations were, in their pre-war form, a national danger.

We cannot allow existing habits and ideas to stand in the way of modern efficiency as the Spitalfields weavers of the South and the Luddites of the Midlands and the North tried to do a hundred years ago, when they wrecked the new machines.

But we must realise that before the war in many industries it was not the workers, but the capitalists who were the machine-wreckers.

Take an imaginary case, an industry producing essential goods. Up to the boom after the last war the industry was a highly competitive and highly profitable affair with falling costs and expanding markets. Then came the big slump and the change in world conditions. By 1929 (if not earlier) the industry found itself unable to compete or, at any rate, unable to compete without drastic overhauls, re-equipment and changes at the top which it did not occur to it to undertake. Instead, the different competing members of the industry got together to protect themselves so far as they could from the consequences of competition. They formed a ring—the Essential Goods Association. Possibly they got a tariff. They arranged a minimum price below which none of their membership was allowed to sell essential goods, even if his costs of production would have permitted him to do so profitably. They raised a fund to deal with what they regarded as their surplus productive plant. They bought it up—and, like the Luddites—they smashed it. They allocated orders for essential goods among themselves according to some agreed rota. They took care not to produce too many essential goods in case their minimum price level might be threatened. It might happen that one or two of the most modern and efficient plants among them were deliberately prevented from operating at full capacity, let alone expanding, in order that the position of the remainder might be preserved and the agreed price of essential goods maintained.

Behind their tariff wall the Essential Goods Association enjoyed the comfort and security of a national market which they farmed like an old-fashioned private estate. Not too much haste, not too much progress, not too much efficiency, not too many new ideas, not too many new men. They didn't really have a plan, just a month-to-month, piecemeal, opportunist habit of action, unrelated to any conception of the future or of national needs. They didn't really have a policy—just an urge to get away from the hazards of free competition, with nothing to put in its place.

This typical industry of ours enjoyed a certain short-term period of prosperity. It had the elementary commonsense or astuteness to offer its workpeople a share in its returns if they would accept a partnership in its restrictive policy. It would do a deal with them —an attractive deal from a limited point of view, but one that would be as fatal to the ultimate aspirations of working people as to the well-being of the whole community.

That is not a fancy picture. It is by and large a perfectly fair account of a substantial fraction of British industry in the period between the two wars; and it reveals a calamitous—a fatal state of affairs. It reveals an industry comfortably dying on its feet and carrying with it into unemployment and decay a growing part of the creative energies of the nation as a whole. For with the decline of industry there went a decline of real enterprise, of thinking, planning, invention—a decline in boldness and the spirit of adventure—a decline in the level of politics, home and foreign, that nearly brought us to destruction. The nation's military potential itself was weakened, so that it found itself years behind the needs of the time in the speed with which and the extent to which its industry could adapt itself to the full demands of modern war. Only the quick abandonment and reversal of this policy of decay, only a partnership between the State and industry which, under the spur of war, revivified and re-energised the failing powers of many of our producers, enabled us to weather the storm and win our way back towards that industrial leadership in war which we were in such danger of losing. With the thunderbolts of war, when they really came, in 1940, there came the lightning flash that revealed what has been happening to our national life and the chance of seeing that the deadly process of decadence was reversed.

A case can be made for private enterprise in appropriate fields. There is—I need not remind this audience—a very powerful case for public enterprise. There is no case whatever for private unenterprise, for private ownership and control without the spur either of a free market and free competition or of real social purpose. In the field of private productive effort security is a dangerous delusion—

an industry which makes security its sole aim is a menace. Unless private enterprise is prepared to take the risks which are its historic function, then private enterprise has no function.

In the post-war world we may have to face the fact of permanent shrinkage in the markets of some of our older industries. I am not suggesting that any policy, however "expansionist", can necessarily expand all industries. I am saying plainly that if central organisation is necessary, whether for contraction, stability, or expansion, the State must exercise genuine and effective control of it.

Let us face the facts that monopolies such as I have described are restrictive in their very essence. That is their reason for existence. You will never alter their nature by patching and tinkering with them—their whole set-up and relation to the community must be profoundly altered. One might argue that a return to free competition would be an appropriate method. But how? Once an industry has reached the state of centralised planning and control represented by these rings and combines you often cannot reverse the trend. Often it is undesirable to do so. Such an omelette can rarely be unscrambled into its constituent eggs.

Still, it may be that in some instances this might be done—by legal changes, by careful public supervision, and by fiscal policies which encourage enterprise. It is, however, beyond doubt that in many instances public action in far more positive forms will be needed. This may sometimes take the form of direct, unsubsidised competition by those Government plants with which the end of the war will leave us so plentifully provided. But in other instances I am convinced that the only answer consistent with national well-being is full and effective public control.

My only hesitation is about that word "control". It sounds restrictive, repressive, damping. The public control that I visualise must be, and given the right men and the right methods it can be, constructive, enlivening, animating.

Here I throw out an idea about the nature of controls. On our industrial controls (by which I do not mean the management of particular businesses) we perhaps need four things represented—expert knowledge of the industry, labour, expert knowledge of the needs and interests of the industry's consumers (whether other industries or the public), and the State. The State should be represented by officers specially trained to understand and work with industry and to know that their duty is to watch the interest of the community as a whole. But, if they have a bias, they should be consumer-minded rather than producer-minded in order to ensure efficient, public-spirited conduct. Moreover, we need, not so much price-control as "efficiency auditing"—a development of cost accounting into a great profession which will be the watchdog of public interest rather than of financial interests in the limited sense.

Thus guided and informed, our monopolies can be made true servants of the public need, true factors in an expanding prosperity. Industrial developments in many countries have shown that an industry which is consciously pursuing social ends, ends of national well-being and welfare, can be as vigorously energised by the pursuit of such ends as ever was a private industry by the spur of competition and the free market.

In such matters of fundamental change, the more there is a general measure of national assent the more secure and successful the change will be. The choice for policy in those monopolised or cartelised industries which are not to be socialised outright is between comfortable, complacent decay, and on the other hand, life, adventure, progress. On the one side is sectional corporatism —or Fascism in its economic forms, however disguised and however politely presented; on the other side a practical mixture of genuine Socialism and genuinely free enterprise, the whole resting upon and in turn supporting national policies of social and industrial welfare.

This, I believe, is the working policy—public ownership where it is appropriate, stimulating public control elsewhere—to which the Socialist ideal commits us as practical men in this age and at this stage. It is a policy that can repel only the reactionary, and will evoke a response among men of all types who share our determination to put the nation and mankind above any sectional interest.

From the very beginning of its history—indeed before its real political history began with the formation of the Labour Representation Committee in 1900—the Labour Movement has been animated by a vision of a unified society reshaped according to the highest conceptions of man's reason and conscience—a vision embracing not only the present and future of our own country but that of the entire human race. The pioneers of the Movement in its early twentieth-century form were men of a lofty moral and social idealism.

That idealism was backed by the driving force of determined millions who knew they were ill used by the economic system and were resolved to better their condition. But the party has never grown, and can never grow, merely from an instinctive thrust for more of this world's goods, animated by no broad conception of universal brotherhood or of a life enriched in far more than the material sense.

My colleague, Ernest Bevin, recently quoted a great labour leader, John Burns, as saying that "the real tragedy of the working class is the poverty of our desires". That was true. In future it must be different. We must not accept for ourselves as a party or for the nation poor desires and limited aims. Abundant life means something far more than, indeed something essentially different from, an abundance of material things. It means more than bread and circuses, more than minimums and movies. It means freedom and fellowship, leisure and the capacity to enjoy it, plenty and the will to share it, an active part in the control of all the affairs which touch men's daily lives; it must mean also soldierly strength and readiness for sacrifice, not only sacrifice of our own lives for our country but sacrifice of some of our own country's immediate and narrower aims and interests in the cause of a wider fellowship.

Upon our British party rests a great responsibility. In 1940 Britain stood as the last bulwark of freedom and progress. All else had gone and she stood alone, yet the flag she held aloft was a flag of victory and it has won through. So with the British Labour Party. It is the last social democratic party to survive in any large country. The others have been overwhelmed by the tides of war and reaction. We are alone, but ours is the winning cause. Labour will again arise in those other lands.

Here, in this island, in our ranks, in the principles that combine democracy and Socialism among us, there stands one of the great hopes of peaceful, rational progress not only for our nation but for the world. It will win through.

The Prime Minister in his broadcast gave us all something to think about in the post-war political field. It is good to think—but not good to jump to precipitate conclusions. Let us turn these matters over well. Let the hysterical and the hasty not seek to commit us one way or the other before we know where our country's need may point us. But one thing I will say, here and now, for all to hear. All my active public life has been spent in this Labour Party of ours. I have played a part in its development. Whether it is in alliance, or whether it is alone, I am of it, for it, with it—and so will remain.